YOUR
MESOPOTAMIA
(ANCIENT IRAQ)

Homework Helper

by John Malam
Consultants: Michael Seymour and Dr. Roger Matthews

ticktock
M E D I A

How to use this book

Each topic in this book is clearly labelled and contains all these components:

Topic heading —

Introduction to the topic

Sub-topic 1 offers complete information about one aspect of the topic

Choose a word from the Keyword Contents on page 3. Then, turn to the correct page and look for your word in BOLD CAPITALS. This will take you straight to the information you need

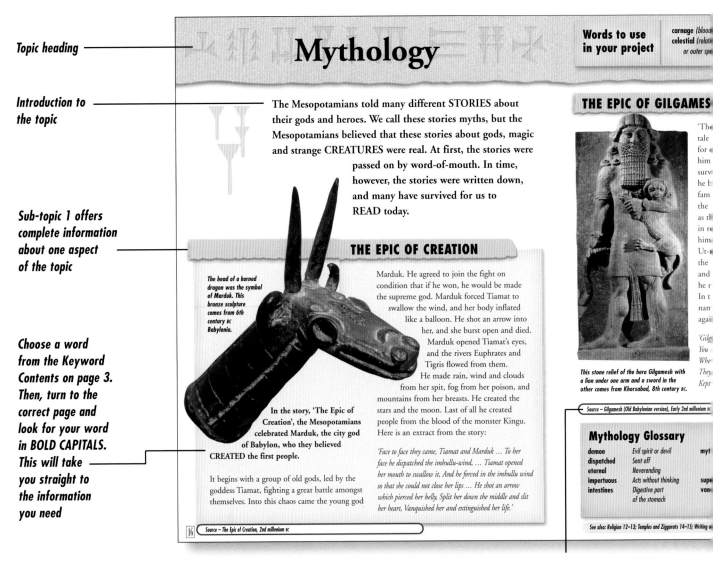

Words to use in your project

carnage (bloo[...]
celestial (relat[...]
or outer spa[...]

Mythology

The Mesopotamians told many different STORIES about their gods and heroes. We call these stories myths, but the Mesopotamians believed that these stories about gods, magic and strange CREATURES were real. At first, the stories were passed on by word-of-mouth. In time, however, the stories were written down, and many have survived for us to READ today.

THE EPIC OF CREATION

The head of a horned dragon was the symbol of Marduk. This bronze sculpture comes from 6th century BC Babylonia.

In the story, 'The Epic of Creation', the Mesopotamians celebrated Marduk, the city god of Babylon, who they believed CREATED the first people.

It begins with a group of old gods, led by the goddess Tiamat, fighting a great battle amongst themselves. Into this chaos came the young god

Marduk. He agreed to join the fight on condition that if he won, he would be made the supreme god. Marduk forced Tiamat to swallow the wind, and her body inflated like a balloon. He shot an arrow into her, and she burst open and died. Marduk opened Tiamat's eyes, and the rivers Euphrates and Tigris flowed from them. He made rain, wind and clouds from her spit, fog from her poison, and mountains from her breasts. He created the stars and the moon. Last of all he created people from the blood of the monster Kingu. Here is an extract from the story:

Face to face they came, Tiamat and Marduk … To her face he dispatched the imhullu-wind, … Tiamat opened her mouth to swallow it, And he forced in the imhullu wind so that she could not close her lips … He shot an arrow which pierced her belly, Split her down the middle and slit her heart, Vanquished her and extinguished her life.'

16 — Source – The Epic of Creation, 2nd millenium BC

THE EPIC OF GILGAMES[...]

'Th[...]
tale[...]
for [...]
him [...]
surv[...]
he b[...]
fam[...]
the [...]
as th[...]
in re[...]
him [...]
Ut-[...]
the [...]
and [...]
he r[...]
In t[...]
nam[...]
agai[...]

'Gilg[...]
You [...]
Whe[...]
They[...]
Kept[...]

This stone relief of the hero Gilgamesh with a lion under one arm and a sword in the other comes from Khorsabad, 8th century BC.

Source – Gilgamesh (Old Babylonian version), Early 2nd millenium BC

Mythology Glossary

demon	Evil spirit or devil
dispatched	Sent off
eternal	Neverending
impertuous	Acts without thinking
intestines	Digestive part of the stomach

myt[...]

sup[...]
van[...]

See also: Religion 12–13; Temples and Ziggurats 14–15; Writing o[...]

The Glossary explains the meaning of any unusual or difficult words appearing on these two pages

Copyright © *ticktock* Entertainment Ltd 2004
First published in Great Britain in 2004 by *ticktock* Media Ltd.,
Unit 2, Orchard Business Centre, North Farm Road, Tunbridge Wells, Kent, TN2 3XF
We would like to thank: Institute of Archaeology at University College London, and Egan-Reid Ltd for their help with this book.
ISBN 1 86007 543 6 HB
ISBN 1 86007 537 1 PB
Printed in China
A CIP catalogue record for this book is available from the British Library.

Sub-topic 2 offers complete information about one aspect of the topic

Some suggested words to use in your project

The Case Study is a closer look at a famous person, artefact or building that relates to the topic

Each photo or illustration is described and discussed in its accompanying text

Captions clearly explain what is in the picture

Other pages in the book that relate to what you have read here are listed in this bar

At the bottom of each section, a reference bar tells you where the quote has come from

epic (long poem)
grotesque (ugly)
immortality (living forever)
moral (aware of right and wrong)
narrative (story)

...ilgamesh' is the
...sh and his search
...This search leads
...shtim, who
...flood because
...for himself, his
...he animals of
...offered sacrifices
...e gods and,
...od Enlil gave
..., Echoes of
...tale survive in
...story of Noah
...As for Gilgamesh,
...eternal life.
...g quote, a woman
...arns Gilgamesh
...t:

...lo you roam?
...e eternal life you seek.
...ed mankind.
...th for mankind,
...heir own hands.'

...raditional story
...ntaining ideas or
...iefs from the past
...ghest or greatest
...nten

...day Life 28–29

CASE STUDY

This clay mask of the demon Humbaba is from Sippar, southern Iraq, about 1800–1600 BC.

Demons and Monsters

The Mesopotamians believed in the existence of **DEMONS** and **MONSTERS**, many of whom appear in their stories. Demons acted as agents of the gods, sent to Earth to punish people. Monsters were hideous creatures. For example, the giant monster Humbaba had a face that looked like a coiled mass of sheep's intestines. According to the Epic of Gilgamesh story, Humbaba was **KILLED** when Gilgamesh chopped his head off. In the following quote, the counsellors of Uruk warn Gilgamesh about the monster Humbaba:

'You are (still young), Gilgamesh, you are impetuous ... But you do not know what you will find ... Humbaba, whose shout is the flood weapon, Whose utterance is fire and whose breath is death, Can hear for up to sixty leagues the sound of his forest.'

Source – Gilgamesh (Standard version), Early-1st millenium BC

Keyword Contents

Mesopotamia

This book is about an area of the ancient world called Mesopotamia, a name which means, 'the land between the rivers'. The rivers are the Euphrates and the Tigris, and the land between them was home to many different communities of people. Today, most of ancient Mesopotamia lies within the borders of IRAQ, with small parts in Turkey and Syria. In ancient times, northern Mesopotamia was called Assyria and the south was called Sumer and, later, Babylonia.

THE LAND AND CLIMATE

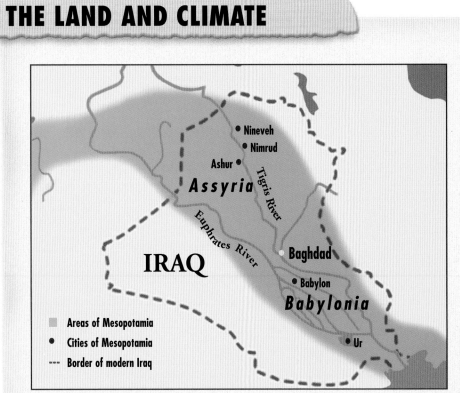

This map shows the main settlements in ancient Mesopotamia.

The region's CLIMATE is hot and arid in summer, cold in winter. There are frequent DUST STORMS, particularly on the flat floodplains between the two rivers.

With little rainfall, people have always lived close to the two rivers. We know exactly where the Mesopotamians lived because archaeologists' excavations have uncovered the remains of many of their cities and villages. Early villages from 8,000–6,000 BC have been excavated as have the first large cities which date from about 3,500 BC. From time to time, both rivers changed their course, cutting new channels across the floodplains. When this happened, settlements could sometimes be washed away.

WHO WERE THE MESOPOTAMIANS?

This glazed tile from the Assyrian city of Nimrud between 883–859 BC shows the Assyrian king Ashurnasirpal II and his attendants.

There were many different **COMMUNITIES** of Mesopotamian people. Some of the major ones were: the Sumerians (3,500–1,900 BC); the Akkadians (2,334–2,150 BC); the Babylonians (1,792–539 BC); and the Assyrians (1,200–612 BC). Information about the different Mesopotamian communities has been gathered from many clay tablets which have been discovered in excavations. For instance, one clay tablet lists the kings of Sumeria. These first kings were believed to have lived for thousands of years:

'When kingship was lowered from heaven … A-lulim (became) king and ruled 28,800 years. Alalgar ruled 36,000 years. Two kings (thus) ruled it for 64,800 years.'

Source – The Sumerian king list, Early-2nd millennium BC

CASE STUDY

This bronze relief decoration shows King Shalmaneser III discovering the source of the River Tigris (c.853 BC).

Euphrates and Tigris Rivers

The peoples of Mesopotamia depended on the two great **RIVERS**. Water was transported to the fields through canals that the Mesopotamians dug across the plains. This technique is known as irrigation, and is still used in the region today. The River Euphrates (1,740 miles long) and the faster flowing River Tigris (1,180 miles long) both **FLOODED** every year between April and June. The importance of the rivers to the Mesopotamians is clear from writings such as this wedding blessing:

'Into the Tigris and Euphrates may flood water be brought, On their banks may the grass grow high, may the meadows be covered, May the holy queen of vegetation pile high the grain heaps and mounds.'

Source – Anonymous, Inanna and the King: wedding night blessing, Early-2nd millennium BC

Mesopotamia Glossary

archaeologists	People who study history by digging up the past		a river floods
arid	Dry like a desert	**irrigation**	System of supplying water through channels
canals	Waterways cut through land	**Mesopotamia**	*(meh-sah-pa-tay-mi-ah)* Ancient name for the area now covered mainly by Iraq
excavations	Digging up ancient objects from the past		
floodplain	Flat area over which	**vegetation**	Plants

See also: Nomads to City Dwellers 6–7; The People 8–9; Warfare 20–21; Farming and Food 22–23

Nomads to City Dwellers

Many important things began or were invented in Mesopotamia. One of the earliest and greatest advances was in FARMING. When the Mesopotamians learned how to take plants and animals from the wild and raise them for their own benefit, they no longer needed to live as nomads, hunting and gathering food from the wild. Instead, they settled down and became the world's first farmers in the world's first villages.

DOMESTICATING PLANTS

Around 9,000 BC, the Mesopotamians started to domesticate two types of WHEAT called 'emmer' and 'einkorn' that they found growing in the wild.

With each new harvest, farmers saved seeds from the best plants, and sowed them the following year. Farmers domesticated other wild plants too. Barley, peas, lentils, carrots, turnips and leeks were all grown by the early Mesopotamians and their neighbours. The Greek writer, Herodotus was amazed by Mesopotamian crops:

'Of all the countries that we know there is none which is so fruitful in grain…. As for the millet and the sesame, I shall not say to what height they grow, though within my own knowledge; for I am not ignorant that what I have already written concerning the fruitfulness of Babylonia must seem incredible to those who have never visited the country.'

Einkorn – a wild variety of wheat – was one of the first plants the Mesopotamian farmers grew as crops.

Source – Herodotus, Histories, Book I, 5th century BC

DOMESTICATING ANIMALS

The early Mesopotamians were also the first people to domesticate wild **ANIMALS**. The first animal they domesticated was probably the dog, which first appeared about 9,000 BC. It was chosen to live and work with people because it was good for hunting. By around 7,000 BC, other wild animals had evolved into domesticated breeds. First and most important was the sheep. Other animals the Mesopotamians domesticated included the pig and the cow. Because they provided food and other resources, people cared a lot about the health and breeding of animals:

'My king, the ewe has given birth to the lamb, The ewe has given birth to the lamb, the ewe has given birth to the good sheep, I will pronounce your name again and again.'

This stone vase decorated with sheep was made about 3,400–3,200 BC.

Source – Hymn to Ninurta as god of fertility and vegetation, 2nd millennium BC

Nomads to City Dwellers Glossary

comprise	Make up parts of a whole	**ignorant**	Lacking knowledge or awareness
domestication	Turning a wild plant or animal into one that can be farmed by humans	**millet**	Type of grain
		nomad	A person who travels from place to place, usually in seasonal movements
evolved	Developed or descended from an earlier form of the same thing		
		scrutinize	Look closely
foundations	Base of a building	**testify**	Confirm proof of something

CASE STUDY

Ishtar Gate is the main gateway to the inner city of Babylon.

Villages, Towns and Cities

As the idea of farming spread, **VILLAGES** appeared throughout Mesopotamia. When the villages grew larger they turned into the world's first **TOWNS**, such as Uruk, which emerged about 3,500 BC. Uruk, now in the desert of south Iraq, was discovered about 100 years ago. As their populations increased, some of the Mesopotamian towns became the world's first **CITIES**. The Mesopotamians were proud of their new way of living, as is clear in the following quote where Gilgamesh, the king of Uruk, shows off his city:

'Go on to the wall of Uruk, Ur-shanabi, and walk around, Inspect the foundation platform and scrutinize the brickwork! Testify that its bricks are baked bricks, And that the Seven Counsellors must have laid its foundations! ... Three square miles and the open ground comprise Uruk.'

See also: Mesopotamia 4–5; The People 8–9; Farming and Food 22–23; Lasting Legacy 30–31

Source – Gilgamesh, Tablet XI, Early-1st millennium BC

The People

As towns and cities began to flourish across Mesopotamia it was necessary to organise the people who lived in them. Mesopotamian SOCIETY was highly structured. At the top of the society were powerful kings, and at the bottom were slaves. In between the two was the great mass of ordinary people. We know a lot about how Mesopotamian society was organised during the time of King Hammurabi, in the 18th century BC. It is the system in Hammurabi's time that is described here.

KINGS – THE RULERS OF MESOPOTAMIA

Because there were many different communities of people in Mesopotamia, there were also many different rulers.

A Mesopotamian ruler was almost always a man. Women could sometimes be very powerful but only in association with **KINGS** and their families. Most of the time, when the king died, one of his sons (usually, but not always, the eldest son) became the new king. The king lived in a palace and was above everyone in the land – except the gods. Many of the kings wrote proud, boastful comments about themselves, such as these words from Shalmaneser III:

'(I am) Shalmaneser, the legitimate king, the king of the world, the king without rival, the "Great Dragon", the (only) power within the four rims (of the earth), overlord of all the princes, who has smashed all his enemies as if (they be) earthenware.'

This is a bronze bust of King Sargon, ruler of Assyria. It dates from about 1,850 BC. It was found at Nineveh.

Source – Shalmaneser III, The fight against the Aramean coalition: Reign of Shalmaneser III, 9th century BC

Words to use in your project

dominant (powerful)	**matrimony** (marriage)
expanded (got bigger)	**monarch** (king or queen)
humanity (people)	**regulations** (laws)

empire (many states ruled by one person)
revered (greatly respected)

COMMONERS, SLAVES, AND WOMEN

The 'Law Code of Hammurabi' clearly set out how the Mesopotamian people were ranked. The first class of people were the 'awilu' (**LANDOWNERS**). Next came the 'mushkenu' (dependants) – who did not own land, but farmed the land owned by the awilu. Last of all came the 'wardu' (**SLAVES**). Mesopotamian **WOMEN** were not considered part of this class-system. They could own land, but few did. Although laws generally favoured men, it was possible for a wife to divorce her husband:

'If a woman so hated her husband that she has declared. "You may not have me," her record shall be investigated at her city council, and if she was careful and was not at fault, even though her husband has been going out and disparaging her greatly, that woman, without incurring any blame at all, may take her dowry and go off to her father's house.'

This terracotta statue of a woman is from Babylonia and dates from about 1,900– 1,700 BC.

Source – The Law Code of Hammurabi, 18th century BC

The People Glossary

devout	Very religious	**earthenware**	Pottery
disparaging	Making insulting comments	**legitimate**	True or worthy of something
dowry	Property or money brought by a bride to her marriage	**oppress**	Treat unfairly
		rival	Someone competing with another

See also: Mesopotamia 4–5; Palaces and Houses 10–11; Writing and Law 18–19; Warfare 20–21

CASE STUDY

This carved head of King Hammurabi is from Susa, 18th century BC.

Hammurabi, a Famous King

Hammurabi was king of Babylon, from 1,728–1,685 BC. When he became king, Babylon was one of many small cities in Mesopotamia. Hammurabi did not want to be remembered as a weak leader so, in the last years of his reign he attacked neighbouring cities and took their land. Hammurabi became the region's most powerful king, and Babylon the leading city. Hammurabi did many good things for his people. He is perhaps best remembered for creating a code of laws that were designed to prevent the strong from taking advantage of the weak. Here is an extract from his **LAW CODE**:

'[The gods] Anum and Enlil named me to promote the welfare of the people, Me, Hammurabi, the devout, god-fearing prince, To cause justice to prevail in the land, To destroy the wicked and the evil, That the strong might not oppress the weak.'

Source – The Law Code of Hammurabi, 18th century BC

Palaces and Houses

The type of house a person lived in depended on his or her STATUS in Mesopotamian society. The king lived in the best house of all – a palace – while his people lived in much smaller homes made from a building material we call mud-brick. The remains of Mesopotamian PALACES from several ancient cities still exist, including those at Mari, Babylon and Nineveh. These, along with ancient writings, enable us to piece together quite a clear picture of where people lived all those thousands of years ago.

PALACES FOR KINGS

A palace was a sign of power and wealth. Some palaces had two storeys, a flat roof, and as many as 300 rooms.

Some rooms were treasuries where the king stored his wealth. Others were workshops where craftsmen made objects for the monarch. The most important room was the king's throne room, where he met visitors and made announcements. This room was sometimes decorated with paintings or stone carvings with images of wars or of the king hunting.

This picture shows the remains of the palace of Nebuchadnezzar II (630–562 BC) at Babylon, Iraq.

The kings were proud of their palaces, as is clear in the following passage:

'(My enemies), whose countries [(are) far away], towards West, [heard] the fame of my rule [… and brought]… gold, silver, … camels and all kinds of spices [to me and kis]sed my feet … I estab[lished] a palace as be[fitting for my position as their king].'

Source – Tiglath-Pileser III, Campaigns Against Syria and Palestine, 8th century BC

Words to use in your project

affluent (rich)	extraordinary (beyond belief)	residence (where someone lives)
construction (building)	lavish (fancy)	
embellish (decorate)	legend (not proven)	symbolic (sign of something)

HOUSES FOR COMMONERS

This Assyrian relief shows builders at work in a village. The relief is from the Palace of Sargon (721–705 BC) at Khorsabad.

Most people lived in small cube-shaped **HOUSES**. Downstairs were rooms for working and receiving visitors. Upstairs were bedrooms and dining rooms. The courtyard was a place to cook food, and where the **FAMILY** could relax. Only the rich could afford bathrooms and toilets, which drained into the river. Most houses, and even the palaces of kings, were built from sun-dried mud-bricks which were good for keeping out the heat. There was one door to the street, sometimes with a frame painted red to keep out evil spirits. An ancient rental agreement describes some details of the agreement:

'A … house belonging to Nana-iddina … [is] at the disposal of Anu-uballit … for 4 shekels of silver as the rent of the house per year … The bareness [of the walls] he shall rectify; the cracks of the walls he shall close up.'

Source – Rent-of-house document, Late-Babylonian period

Palaces and Houses Glossary

agreement	Legally binding document	Seven Wonders of the World	Seven most amazing man-made structures of ancient world
courtyard	An open-air space enclosed by walls		
disposal	Welcome to be used	shekel	Silver coin used as money in Mesopotamia
mud-brick	A rectangular brick made from mud	treasuries	Storerooms where valuables were kept
rectify	Fix		

See also: Mesopotamia 4–5; The People 8–9; Farming and Food 22–23; Everyday Life 28–29

CASE STUDY

Some believe these are the foundations of the Hanging Gardens of Babylon in Iraq. Others believe the gardens never existed.

Hanging Gardens of Babylon

The most famous royal palace was built in the city of Babylon by King Nebuchadnezzar II who reigned from 630–562 BC. It is best known today for its so-calllled 'Hanging Gardens'. The ancient writer Philo named the **GARDENS** as one of the Seven Wonders of the World. He wrote:

'The Hanging Garden with its plants above the ground grows in the air. The roots of trees above form a roof over the ground. Stone pillars stand under the garden to support it.'

Some people think the story of the Hanging Gardens is a myth. It is an unsolved **MYSTERY**.

Source – Philo, 3rd century BC

Religion

The Mesopotamians were a highly religious people who worshipped many different GODS and GODDESSES. They believed people had been created to serve the gods, working for them as their servants on Earth. People thought that if they served the gods well, they would be protected from harm. However, if they did not look after the gods, bad things might happen – such as floods, drought, disease, or attacks from enemies.

GODS AND GODDESSES

Gods and goddesses were thought to be beings with superhuman POWERS.

There were as many as 3,000 different deities worshipped in Mesopotamia – but not all by the same communities. Many written tributes to the gods survive, such as the Hymn to Ishtar:

'Praise Ishtar, the most awesome of the goddesses, … The fate of everything she holds in her hand. At her glance there is created joy, Power, magnificence, the protecting deity and guardian spirit.'

This double statue of the god Adad and goddess Ishtar from the 9th century BC was discovered at Tell Halaf, Syria.

Source – Hymn to Ishtar, 1,600 BC

HYMNS AND PRAYERS

Priests composed 'hymns' which were sacred **SONGS** that praised the gods and thanked them for their kindness. Many of these hymns have survived as written clay tablets. Hymns were spoken, or sung to music that was played on instruments such as the harp. **PRAYERS** were offered to the gods for many different reasons. People with poor health asked to be made better; those with enemies asked to be kept safe from harm; those with no food asked to be fed, and so on. Here is an extract from a Mesopotamian hymn:

'O my god, (my) transgressions are seven times seven; remove my transgressions; O my godess, (my) transgressions are seven times seven; remove my transgressions; … Remove my transgressions and I will sing thy praise.'

This Sumerian statuette shows a person in prayer.

Source – Prayer to every god, 7th century BC

Religion Glossary

deity	*A god or a goddess*	**superhuman**	*Having powers greater than a normal human being*
drought	*A long period of no rainfall*		
hymn	*Religious song that honours the gods*	**transgressions**	*Breaking rules*
		tribute	*Act or gift that shows gratitude or respect*
purification	*Cleansing ceremony*		

CASE STUDY

This limestone plaque showing people bearing offerings to the gods comes from Ur, southern Iraq, about 2,500–2,300 BC.

Holy Days and Festivals

Certain days were holy days, or times when religious **FESTIVALS** were held. These were important events, when the gods were praised and celebrated. In return for their public displays of love, respect and loyalty, people hoped the gods would protect their towns, and provide them with food. Many holy days and festivals were connected with farming, such as the festival of 'akitu' – a thanksgiving festival for the barley harvest and a celebration for the start of a new year. Here is an extract from a temple purification performed during this New Year festival at Babylon:

'When it is two hours after sunrise, … purify the temple and sprinkle water, (taken from) … the Tigris and … the Euphrates, on the temple. He [the priest] shall beat the kettle-drum inside the temple. He shall have a censer and a torch brought into the temple...'.

Source – Temple programme for the New Year's festival at Babylon, 3rd century BC

See also: Palaces and Houses 10–11; Temples and Ziggurats 14–15; Mythology 16–17; Science and Medicine 26–27

Temples and Ziggurats

Every Mesopotamian town and city had a temple building – and sometimes many of them. A temple was built to HONOUR the community's main god, and was a very important place. As the years passed, the temple developed into many religious buildings, spread out over a large area. Some temple complexes contained another important building, a PYRAMID-shaped tower called a 'ziggurat'.

TEMPLES

A Mesopotamian temple was not a meeting place for WORSHIPPERS. Instead, it was a house on Earth where the spirit of a god was thought to live:

'Bright light, god Marduk, who dwells in the temple Eudul, … To your city, Babylon, grant release! … At your exalted command, O lord of the great gods, Let light be set before the people of Babylon.'

As well as the temple building, the complex included living areas for **PRIESTS** and temple workers. There were also open-air courtyards where worshippers gathered on holy days and at festivals, and store rooms where valuables and grain were kept. A temple was a busy place, with people coming and going all day long. The entire temple complex was surrounded by a high wall.

The Mesopotamian Ziggurat at Ur is the most famous example of a Mesopotamian ziggurat.

Source – Temple program for the New Year's festival at Babylon, 3rd century BC

Words to use in your project

dedicated *(devote to)*
divine *(godly)*
hygiene *(cleanliness)*

inhabit *(live inside)*
magnificent *(grand)*
monument *(structure)*

protocol *(rules of behaviour)*
significant *(very important)*
toil *(hard work)*

ZIGGURATS

The most famous type of Mesopotamian building is the 'ziggurat' which means 'high place'. One of the best examples is the ziggurat at Ur in south Iraq, from 2,000 BC. A ziggurat stood on its own, or within a temple complex. It was a pyramid-shaped tower of several flat platforms, built one on top of the other. The platforms were reached by ramps and staircases on the outside of the building. There were no rooms or passages inside a ziggurat – it was a solid block of millions of mud-bricks, held together with wooden beams and reed matting. It would have taken a long time to build a ziggurat, as is clear from the following extract:

This is the ziggurat at Aqarquf, near Baghdad.

'The Annunaki [people] began shovelling, For a whole year they made bricks for it, When the second year arrived, … They had built a high ziggurat.'

Source – The Epic of Creation, Tablet VI, Early-2nd millenium BC

Temples and Ziggurats Glossary

complex	Group of buldings
deities	Gods and goddesses
exalted	Very happy
platforms	Levels or storeys of a building
priests/priestesses	Religious leaders
sacrifice	Killing an animal as an offering to the gods
temple	Building for worshipping or honouring the gods
ziggurat	A pyramid with steps up its sides leading to flat platforms and a temple

CASE STUDY

Figure of a temple priest from Palace of Sargon at Khorsabad.

Priests and Priestesses

Priests, who were men, tended to work at temples dedicated to gods; while **PRIESTESSES**, who were women, usually worked at temples dedicated to goddesses. Both had shaved heads, which was a sign of cleanliness. Their duties were to serve the temple deity. Twice a day they took gifts of food to the sacred statue, where the god or goddesses was believed to live, and dressed it in clean clothes. At festivals they paraded the statue in the courtyard for worshippers to see. Sometimes they carried the statue to temples in other towns, so the god could visit other gods. Sometimes priests and priestesses **SACRIFICED ANIMALS** to the gods:

'Every day throughout the year, ten fat, clean rams, whose horns and hooves are whole, shall be sacrificed … to the deities Anu and Antu of heaven, to the planets Jupiter, Venus, Mercury, Saturn, and Mars, to the sunrise, and to the appearance of the moon.'

Source – Daily sacrifices to the gods of the city of Uruk, 3rd century BC

See also: Palaces and Houses 10–11; Religion 12–13; Mythology 16–17; Science and Medicine 26–27

Mythology

The Mesopotamians told many different STORIES about their gods and heroes. We call these stories myths, but the Mesopotamians believed that these stories about gods, magic and strange CREATURES were real. At first, the stories were passed on by word-of-mouth. In time, however, the stories were written down, and many have survived for us to READ today.

The head of a horned dragon was the symbol of Marduk. This bronze sculpture comes from 6th century BC Babylonia.

In the story, 'The Epic of Creation', the Mesopotamians celebrated Marduk, the city god of Babylon, who they believed CREATED the first people.

It begins with a group of old gods, led by the goddess Tiamat, fighting a great battle amongst themselves. Into this chaos came the young god

THE EPIC OF CREATION

Marduk. He agreed to join the fight on condition that if he won, he would be made the supreme god. Marduk forced Tiamat to swallow the wind, and her body inflated like a balloon. He shot an arrow into her, and she burst open and died. Marduk opened Tiamat's eyes, and the rivers Euphrates and Tigris flowed from them. He made rain, wind and clouds from her spit, fog from her poison, and mountains from her breasts. He created the stars and the moon. Last of all he created people from the blood of the monster Kingu. Here is an extract from the story:

'Face to face they came, Tiamat and Marduk … To her face he dispatched the imhullu-wind, … Tiamat opened her mouth to swallow it, And he forced in the imhullu wind so that she could not close her lips … He shot an arrow which pierced her belly, Split her down the middle and slit her heart, Vanquished her and extinguished her life.'

Source – The Epic of Creation, 2nd millennium BC

THE EPIC OF GILGAMESH

This stone relief of the hero Gilgamesh with a lion under one arm and a sword in the other comes from Khorsabad, 8th century BC.

'The Epic of Gilgamesh' is the tale of Gilgamesh and his search for eternal life. This search leads him to Ut-napishtim, who survived a great flood because he built a boat for himself, his family, and all the animals of the world. He offered sacrifices as thanks to the gods and, in return, the god Enlil gave him eternal life. Echoes of Ut-napishtim's tale survive in the Bible as the story of Noah and the flood. As for Gilgamesh, he never gained eternal life. In the following quote, a woman named Siduri warns Gilgamesh against his quest:

'Gilgamesh, where do you roam?
You will not find the eternal life you seek.
When the gods created mankind.
They appointed death for mankind,
Kept eternal life in their own hands.'

Source – Gilgamesh (Old Babylonian version), Early-2nd millennium BC

Mythology Glossary

demon	*Evil spirit or devil*	**myth**	*A traditional story containing ideas or beliefs from the past*
dispatched	*Sent off*		
eternal	*Neverending*		
impetuous	*Acts without thinking*	**supreme**	*Highest or greatest*
intestines	*Digestive part of the stomach*	**vanquished**	*Beaten*

CASE STUDY

This clay mask of the demon Humbaba is from Sippar, southern Iraq, about 1,800–1,600 BC.

Demons and Monsters

The Mesopotamians believed in the existence of **DEMONS** and **MONSTERS**, many of whom appear in their stories. Demons acted as agents of the gods, sent to Earth to punish people. Monsters were hideous creatures. For example, the giant monster Humbaba had a face that looked like a coiled mass of sheep's intestines. According to the Epic of Gilgamesh story, Humbaba was **KILLED** when Gilgamesh chopped his head off. In the following quote, the counsellors of Uruk warn Gilgamesh about the monster Humbaba:

'You are (still young), Gilgamesh, you are impetuous ... But you do not know what you will find ... Humbaba, whose shout is the flood weapon, Whose utterance is fire and whose breath is death, Can hear for up to sixty leagues the sound of his forest.'

Source – Gilgamesh (Standard version), Early-1st millenium BC

See also: Religion 12–13; Temples and Ziggurats 14–15; Writing and Law 18–19; Everyday Life 28–29

Writing and Law

Writing was invented by the Sumerians, who lived in southern Mesopotamia around 3,000 BC. Their brilliant invention is a milestone in the history of humankind, and allowed the Mesopotamian culture to PROGRESS greatly. Through their writings, we can learn about the Mesopotamians first hand through their own words. Mesopotamian texts range from simple lists of goods, to complex stories and the laws that governed the way their society was run.

PICTURES AND SOUNDS

This necklace bead bears a cuneiform inscription belonged to Mesanepada, King of Hur Mari, from about 2,500 BC.

The first kind of writing used by the Mesopotamians was PICTURE writing. It used pictures to represent things.

We call them 'pictograms'. A picture of a sheep meant 'one sheep', and a sheep with two circles beside it would mean 'two sheep'. This type of writing was invented to record the business activities of farmers and merchants. However, picture writing was limited, as it could only be used for object words. It could not be used for all the words in the Mesopotamian language. Other words were written as **SYMBOLS**. We call such symbols 'phonograms'. Writing developed to help keep financial and administrative records, such as this one:

'Marduk-remani the scribe … has received 23 kur 5 sut of dates as a partial payment from the hands of Arad-Bel … (he) has entered this partial payment … on the writing board … and will show it to Iddin-Bel and Nabu-eber-napshati.'

Source – Temple administrative document (payment for scribe Marduk-remani), 5th–4th century BC

WRITING ON CLAY

The Mesopotamians did not write on paper. Instead, they wrote on pieces of soft **CLAY** which we call 'clay tablets'. To write on clay, a scribe held a tablet in the palm of one hand. The back of the tablet was rounded to fit the hollow of his palm. The face of the tablet was flat, which is what the scribe wrote on with a 'stylus' made from the cut stem of a water reed. A scribe wrote in lines from left to right, or from top to bottom. When he had finished, the tablet was left to dry in the sun, or baked hard in an oven. The writing looks like clusters of wedge-shaped marks. Therefore, the name we give to this kind of

Mesopotamian wedge-writing is 'cuneiform', which is Latin for 'wedge-shaped'.

This 13th century BC clay tablet from El Quitar, Syria (bottom) shows the cuneiform script. The clay outer envelope (top) protected the contents from being altered.

Writing and Law Glossary

cuneiform	*Mesopotamian wedge-shaped writing*		*'writing in pictures'*
		partial	*Part of a whole*
phonogram	*From a Greek word meaning 'writing in sounds'*	**scribe**	*A person trained to read and write*
		stylus	*A writing instrument*
pictogram	*From a Greek word meaning*	**tablet**	*Flat slab of clay used for writing*

CASE STUDY

Law

Mesopotamian **LAWS** were often written on clay tablets. They were also carved on blocks of stone that were put up in public places for everyone to see. Most people could not read or write, and so important documents would be read aloud in front of crowds of people. The most famous example of a set of laws is the 'Law Code of Hammurabi'. It is a list of 282 laws carved in 3,500 lines of cuneiform writing onto a block of hard black stone. The stone is 2.2m (7.5ft) tall and weighs 4 tonnes. Hammurabi's laws were organised into sections dealing with the family, work, property, land, prices and wages, slavery and trade. The laws were designed to be **FAIR** to all, but they include many harsh **PUNISHMENTS**. Here are three examples of these laws:

'If a son hits his father, his hand shall be cut off; ... If a man puts out a man's eye, his own eye shall be put out; ... If a man breaks a man's bone, he shall pay him a sum of silver.'

The Law Code of Hammurabi was inscribed on this plaque from Chaldea in the 18th century BC.

See also: The People 18–19; Arts and Crafts 24–25; Science and Medicine 26–27; Lasting Legacy 30–31

Source – Law Code of Hammurabi, 18th century BC

Warfare

Wars were fought throughout the history of Mesopotamia. They began when one community did something to OFFEND another. For example, if a city tried to take control of another city's water supply, the two might go to war. Other reasons might be if a king INVADED his neighbour's land, stole or damaged his property or insulted his gods. In a land where access to WATER was essential for growing crops, much conflict occurred over water rights.

THE ARMY

King Sargon of Akkad (who reigned from 2,340–2,125 BC) formed the first army of full-time SOLDIERS.

The army included men who fought at close range with spears and swords, archers who fired arrows from a distance, messengers and spies. Engineers built equipment such as battering-rams to break down the walls of enemy cities. **FORTUNE-TELLERS** were also part of the army. Their job was to sacrifice animals and inspect their entrails, looking for omens about the king's military plan. Records of Mesopotamian warfare exist in the form of stone slabs from the palaces at Nineveh and Nimrud, as well as written descriptions from kings:

'As to Hanno of Gaza … who had fled before my army and run away to Egypt, [I conquered] the town of Gaza … [and I placed the images of] my [gods] and my royal image in his own palace … and declared [them] to be … the gods of their country.'

The Royal Standard of Ur features images of the Sumerian army with chariots.

Source – Tiglath-pileser III, 744–727 BC

Words to use in your project

campaign *(military operation)*	or respect)
expeditions *(trips)*	**heroic** *(very brave)*
formidable *(inspiring fear*	**instigate** *(start something)*

siege *(when an army surrounds their enemy until they surrender)*

WEAPONS AND ARMOUR

The main **WEAPONS** of the Mesopotamian armies were the spear and the bow and arrow. Other types of weapons included spears, javelins, maces, axes, daggers, slings, and swords with long, curved blades. Soldiers wore leather or metal helmets to protect their heads.

Metal armour was made from hundreds of tiny pieces of bronze that overlapped each other, like fish scales, sewn to a leather or cloth tunic. Mesopotamian weapons are clearly described by the Greek writer Herodotus:

'The Assyrians went to war with helmets upon their heads made of brass, and plaited in a strange fashion which is not easy to describe. They carried shields, lances, and daggers very like the Egyptian; but in addition they had wooden clubs knotted with iron, and linen corselets.'

This copper axe (far left) was found in one of the royal graves of Ur and is from about 2,600–2,400 BC. The bronze sword (left) is from the Kassite dynasty, about 1,400–1,100 BC.

Source – Herodotus, Histories, 5th century BC

Warfare Glossary

bespattered	*Splattered with liquid*	**entrails**	*The insides of an animal*
conflict	*Fighting or warfare*	**lances**	*Long weapon like a sword*
corselets	*Type of armour*	**omen**	*A sign taken to mean*
engineer	*Person who designs and builds things*		*what will happen in the future*

See also: Mesopotamia 4–5; Farming and Food 22–23; Arts and Crafts 24–25; Lasting Legacy; 31–31

CASE STUDY

This 8th century BC basalt Assyrian stele from Tell Ahama shows warriors riding in a chariot.

The Chariot

Two-wheeled **CHARIOTS** were an important feature of Mesopotamian armies. Fast and lightweight, they were the chief fighting vehicle of their time. The chariot was a platform on wheels led by horses and steered by a driver. An archer would fire arrows from the platform. Some chariots held up to four archers. Some also carried a 'bodyguard' whose job was to protect the archer by holding a shield in front of him. Chariots were also used on hunting trips. Sennacherib described his bloody battle ride by chariot in a war against Elam:

'My prancing steeds, harnessed for my riding, plunged into the streams of their blood ... The wheels of my war chariot ... were bespattered with blood and filth.'

Source – Annals of Sennacherib (Late-8th century BC)

Farming and Food

FARMERS were very important to Mesopotamian society. More people worked on the land growing crops, tending to animals, and looking after the water supply than in any other occupation. In the north of the region farmers relied on rainfall to water their fields. In the drier south, water was channelled to fields by irrigation canals. The digging and clearing of canals were extremely important public duties for all citizens, in order to make their lands more fertile.

CROPS, BREAD AND BEER

The most important crop for farmers was barley. Its grains were ground into flour to make **BREAD**.

Milk, butter, cheese, fruit and sesame seeds could be added to make different kinds of bread. Barley was also used to make a low-alcohol **BEER**, drunk through straws to avoid hard bits being swallowed. Onions and garlic were the main **VEGETABLES**, along with lettuces, cabbages, carrots and cucumbers. Fruit crops included apples, cherries, figs, pears, plums and dates. Water was crucial to growing everything, as described below:

'In days of yore a farmer gave (these) instructions to his son: When you are about to cultivate your field, take care to open the irrigation works (so that) their water does not rise too high in the field. When you have emptied it of water, watch the field's wet ground that it stays even: let no wandering ox trample it.'

This detail of the Warka Vase from Uruk, about 3,500–3,000 BC, shows people bearing food.

Source – Farmer's Instructions, 1,700 BC

Words to use in your project

livelihood *(way of living)*
orchard *(group of fruit trees)*
preserving *(way of treating*

food so it doesn't go rotten)
staple *(main food in a society)*
sustenance *(food and drink)*

seasoning *(flavouring)*
trapping *(catching animals in traps)*

ANIMALS

This terracotta seal from the 2nd millennium BC is from the Syrian city of Mari and shows a man with deer which would have been farmed for their meat.

The main farm animals were **CATTLE** and goats (which both provided milk) and **SHEEP**. Sheep provided wool, and cattle hides were made into leather – both were then used to make clothes. The Mesopotamians also ate the meat from pigs, sheep, deer and cattle.

Ducks, geese and hens were farmed for their eggs, as well as meat. Oxen and donkeys were the main draught animals, pulling carts and ploughs and helping around the farm:

'Once the sky constellations are right, do not be reluctant to take the oxen force to the field many times.'

Source – Farmer's Almanac, 1,700 BC

Farming and Food Glossary

canals	*Man-made waterways*	**fertile**	*Rich soil that produces good crops*
constellations	*Groups of stars*		
cultivate	*Grow crops or plants*	**gazelles**	*Small deer-like animal*
delicacy	*Special treat*	**irrigation**	*Channelling water to crops*
draught	*Pulling something*	**occupation**	*Job*

See also: Mesopotamia 4–5; Nomads to City Dwellers 6–7; Everyday Life 28–29; Lasting Legacy 30–31

CASE STUDY

Fishing and Hunting

People also ate wild food – especially fish. They were caught in the Tigris and Euphrates rivers, in lakes, and in the Mediterranean and Gulf seas. Teams of **FISHERMEN** trapped them in large nets and pulled them ashore. Some worked alone, hooking fish with rods and lines, and with small nets. Fish could be eaten fresh, or preserved by salting or smoking. Hares, birds and gazelles were **HUNTED** for their meat. Even locusts were caught in Babylon – where they were enjoyed as a crunchy insect delicacy.

'The sea was filled with carp and … fish, … The forests were filled with deer and wild goats, … The watered gardens were filled with (honey) and wine.'

This Assyrian relief from Nineveh, in about 650 BC shows men hunting with dogs and cages.

Source – Hymn to Ninurta as god of fertility and vegetation, 2nd millennium BC

23

Arts and Crafts

The people of Mesopotamia who practised crafts used a wide range of raw materials. They made ordinary everyday items, luxury goods and art objects. It is believed that craft workers were always men, and that fathers passed their SKILLS on to their sons, from one generation to the next. By studying the objects they made, we can find out how they were made, what tools were used to make them, and about the society from which they came.

METAL OBJECTS

Copper, BRONZE and iron were the main metals used for everyday objects, such as kitchen equipment, weapons, statues, and parts for chariots and furniture.

GOLD and silver were used for decorative and high-quality items, such as JEWELLERY. As Mesopotamia lacked the raw materials ('ores') that produce metals, they had to be brought in from outside the region. Red-hot copper and bronze were poured into moulds of clay or stone, to cast axes, daggers and spearheads. Casting was also used for gold and silver items. Iron needed higher temperatures and could not be shaped by casting. Instead, it was heated in a forge, then beaten into shape. Vessels made of precious metals were used for offering food to the gods:

'Every day in the year, for the main meal of the morning, you shall prepare ... eighteen gold vessels ... (filled with various kinds of beer) on the tray of the god Anu.'

This gold headdress is from the Royal Cemetery at Ur, from about 2,600 BC.

Source – Daily Sacrifices to the Gods of the City of Uruk, 2nd millennium BC

CLAY, GLASS AND IVORY

POTTERY-making was the most common Mesopotamian craft. Clay was found across the region, and potters shaped it into bowls, plates, saucers and jars. The first pots were handmade. Then, after about 4,500 BC pots were made on a slowly spinning wheel which allowed potters to make pots in different shapes. Glass-making was very skilled work. Around 1,600 BC the Mesopotamians learned how to make hollow glass objects, such as **VASES** and bottles. Many fine objects and raw materials came into Mesopotamian cities as war-booty:

'I carried away as booty his ... possessions in large amounts ... gold, silver, precious stones, elephant-hides, ivory, ebony and boxwood, garments (made) with multicoloured trimmings and linen, all his personal valuables.'

Dating back to the Kassite dynasty (about 1,300–1,200 BC), this glass bottle was found in a grave at Ur.

Source – Esarhaddon, Syro-Palestinian Campaign, 680-669 BC

Arts and Crafts Glossary

booty	Goods stolen in wars	**ivory**	Hard, creamy-white material that comes from elephant tusks
cylinder	3D-shape with straight sides and a curved end		
cast	When an object is made by shaping it in a mould	**mould**	A hollow shape in which an object is cast
effaces	Rubs off	**ore**	The raw material from which metal is obtained
forge	A furnace in which metal is heated until it is soft enough to shape	**vessel**	Hollow container for holding liquid

See also: Writing and Law 18–19; Warfare 20–21; Farming and Food 22–23; Everyday Life 28–29

CASE STUDY

Objects Made of Stone

Stonemasons carved life-size **STATUES** of kings, and scenes of hunts and battles that decorated the walls of royal palaces. Stone was also used for 'cylinder seals' – tiny cylinder-shaped objects with finely carved surfaces. When rolled over a clay pad fixed to an item of property, a cylinder seal left an impression, or print, of its pattern. The pattern was a 'signature' stamp that identified the owner of the property. Here are Sennacherib's instructions for the making of his seal:

'You will write ... upon the (stone) tablet-seal ... as follows: Palace of Sennacherib, king ... Who(ever) effaces my inscribed name, ... may the gods Ashur, Sin, Shamash, Adad (and) Ishtar ... remove his descendents from the land of stone.'

White and cream cylinder seal from Uruk, southern Iraq. About 3,200–3,100 BC.

Source – Sennacherib's instructions for inscribing his seal, 714–681 BC

Science and Medicine

The Mesopotamians were interested in the WORLD around them, and they searched for ways to understand and explain it. We know they studied MATHEMATICS, astronomy and medicine because clay tablets have been found which explore different ideas about many subjects. Scientific study was usually carried out by priests, who interpreted what they saw in relation to the gods.

MATHEMATICS AND NUMERACY

This is a clay tablet that shows an account of goats and sheep, from Tellohc, Sumeria, about 2,350 BC.

Mathematics developed in Mesopotamia from about 3,000 BC, soon after the invention of writing.

It came about due to the need to keep accurate numbers of such things as how much grain was produced and how many sheep a farmer had.

The most widely used number system was based on counting in units of 60. This is called a 'sexagesimal' system. They also invented another counting system, based on **COUNTING** in tens, hundreds, and thousands. This is called the 'decimal system', which is still used today. One everyday use of mathematics was calculating rations of food:

'A certain Buzi [name] at 120 qu, 4 workmen at 60 qu, 2 female slaves at 30 qu, 2 sons at 30 qu, 2 sons at 20 qu, 2 daughters at 20 qu, [making] 1 kur 260 qu of barley for rations per month.'

Source – Receipt of barley for rations, Early 2nd millennium BC

ASTRONOMY AND ASTROLOGY

The Sumerians were the first people to describe the Milky Way.

To the Mesopotamians, astronomy and astrology were closely related. Priests observed the night sky with their naked eyes (they had no telescopes) and made detailed records of the positions of stars, planets and the phases of the moon. They believed that the positions of the **STARS** and **PLANETS** acted as omens for people on Earth. People made many astronomical observations:

'From the 15th day of the (3rd) month Simanu daylight converts to night-time, the days become shorter, the nights become longer ...',

but often explained what they saw in terms of gods:

'Holy Inanna was endowed by Enlil and Ninlil with the power to turn light to darkness and darkness to light.'

Source – Old Babylonian document about Inanna, Early-2nd millennium BC

Science and Medicine Glossary

astrology	The study of how stars and planets affect people's lives		based on units of 10
		incantation	A set of words spoken or sung as a magic spell
astronomy	The study of stars and planets	**ointment**	Lotion or cream for rubbing on body
converts	Changes into something else	**omens**	Sign which tells the future
decimal	A system of counting	**sexagesimal**	A system of counting based on units of 60

See also: Religion 12–13; Temples and Ziggurats 14–15; Writing and Law 18–19; Lasting Legacy 30–31

CASE STUDY

Medicine and Magic

When a person fell **ILL**, they chose whether to be seen by a medical doctor ('asu') or a doctor who used **MAGIC** ('ashipu'). The ashipu doctor sometimes used spells and incantations. The asu doctor made medicines and ointments from plants and minerals. Here is a doctor's remedy for pain in the ears:

'If the inside of the ears of a man hurt ... you prepare a perfume (using) separately oil from kanaktu, oil from "sweet-reed", cypress oil, and mix them together, you apply it into his ear, (and then) you wrap a lump of salt in a wad of wool and put it into his ear.'

This stone tablet of Gula, the goddess of medicine, comes from Susa, Iran, from about 1,300 BC.

Source – Medical text, 6th century BC

27

Everyday Life

There is a variety of evidence that survives to help us build a picture of everyday life in Mesopotamia. Excavations have revealed childhood TOYS and games, while statues, wall carvings and decorative objects give us an idea of the clothes people wore. We even know what their music was like from the world's oldest examples of 'sheet music', and by the many musical instruments that have been discovered by archaeologists.

TOYS AND GAMES

Babies shook RATTLES made of baked clay filled with pebbles. Older children played with wooden BALLS, skipping ropes and spinning tops, and models of animals, furniture and chariots.

Older children also played with a 'buzzer' toy – a clay disc with two holes through it, rather like a big button. A string passed through the holes, and was held at each end and twisted until it was tight. When the tension was released the string unwound, the disc whirled around at speed which made a buzzing noise. Adults liked to play **BOARD GAMES**. A game for two players was found in a royal tomb in the city of Ur. Made about 2,500 BC, it is a board of 21 squares. The game was a 'passing' game, where each player had to move their counters past their opponent's to reach the opposite end of the board. Each player had seven counters.

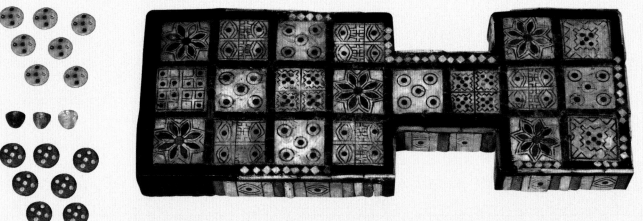

The Royal Game of Ur was found in the royal cemetery at Ur. It dates back to about 2,600–2,400 BC.

Words to use in your project

attire *(clothes)*	**cosmetics** *(make-up)*	**fashionable** *(stylish)*
chorus *(large group of singers)*	**entertainment** *(fun)*	**pastimes** *(hobbies)*
compose *(write music)*	**fabric** *(cloth material)*	**recreation** *(leisure time)*

CLOTHING, HAIR AND MAKE-UP

Around 2,500 BC, men wore short, plain kilts held in place by a belt or knot, and their chests were bare. Women wore long tunics, wrapped around the body and pinned at the chest. A thousand years later, men wore tunics that reached to the knee or ankle, as did the women who also wore shawls to cover their shoulders. Early on, **CLOTHES** were made from wool, but linen became the main fabric in later times. In this example, a shopkeeper defends her products to a complaining customer:

'Why do you keep on writing to me: "the textiles that you send me are always of bad quality!" Who is the man who lives in your house and criticises the textiles that are brought to him?'

By 1,000 BC it was fashionable for men and women to wear their **HAIR** in long, tight curls, and men had pointed beards. Women wore **MAKE-UP** – such as 'antimony' for mascara and eyeliner and red henna for lipstick and blusher.

This limestone statuette of a bearded man wearing a tunic is from Tell Asmar, Iraq, 3rd millennium BC.

Source – Letter written by Lamassi, Early-2nd millennium BC

CASE STUDY

This lyre was found in Queen Pu-abi's grave at the royal cemetery at Ur. It dates from about 2,600-2,400 BC.

Music and Song

Clay tablets have been found with musical notes written on them (the world's oldest examples of 'sheet music'). **MUSIC** was played on harps and lyres (stringed instruments), pipes, flutes, horns (wind instruments), and drums, cymbals, castanets, bells and rattles (percussion instruments). People sang songs about love and work, and hymns that praised the gods. Even the myths of the Mesopotamians were put to music and sung. An ancient table gives advice for tuning a sammu-harp:

'If the sammu is tuned to X and the (interval) Y is not clear, you tighten the string N and Y will be clear.'

Source – Document from Ur, 2nd millennium BC

Everyday Life Glossary

antimony	Brittle blue-black metal used for making women's make-up	**henna**	A reddish-brown dye obtained from the henna plant
castanets	Small pieces of wood clicked together to make music	**lyre**	A string instrument with two upright posts (a harp has one post only)
cymbals	Brass plates struck with a stick to make music	**textiles**	Material that clothing is made from

See also: The People 8–9; Palaces and Houses 10–11; Farming and Food 22–23; Arts and Crafts 24–25

Lasting Legacy

There are many things in today's world which can be traced back to Mesopotamia, such as farming methods, writing and cities. The Mesopotamians left many stories such as the tale of Ut-napishtim, who you can read about in the Book of Genesis in the Bible, where he is called Noah. Even the Bible story of the first Christmas can be linked to Mesopotamia, since the three wise men, or 'magi', who travelled from the east were probably Mesopotamian astronomer-priests.

THE INVENTION OF THE WHEEL

The Mesopotamians invented the WHEEL – one of the greatest inventions ever. The earliest wheels were probably pottery spinning wheels which date back to around 4,700 BC.

The first vehicles had wheels which were solid and made from two or three wooden planks shaped into disks. The planks were joined together with wooden or copper brackets. Solid wheels were used for more than 1,000 years, until around 2,000 BC when wheels with spokes started to be made. As wheeled vehicles became the main means of **TRANSPORT**, roads developed between towns, along which oxen pulled carts. **ROADS** also allowed kings and their armies to move around more quickly, making war and demanding tribute:

'I departed from Carchemish, taking the road between the mountains … I advanced towards the town Hazazu … There I received gold and linen garments (as tribute).'

This chariot model comes from the city of Ur, from the Babylonian period (about 2,000–1,600 BC).

Source – Ashurnasirpal II, 883-859 BC

Words to use in your project

astrology *(the study of how stars and planets influence human beings)*

astronomy *(science of stars, planets and the universe)*

innovation *(invention)*

meticulous *(very thorough)*
network *(systemn of roads)*
spherical *(circular)*

COUNTING IN 60S

The Mesopotamian custom of counting in 60s is still in use today. For example, when we measure **TIME** we count 60 seconds in a minute and 60 minutes in an hour. Dividing the day into 12 daytime hours and 12 night-time hours is also thought to have been a Mesopotamian **INVENTION**. In geometry (a branch of mathematics that deals with lines, angles and solids) we divide a circle into 360 equal parts or degrees, which is a multiple of 60 (6 x 60 = 360).

'The division of the day into twelve parts (was) received by the Greeks from the Babylonians.'

The Mesopotamians invented time-keeping as we know it today. This 17th-century German watch shows the days of the week, months, zodiac and phases of the moon in Arabic symbols.

Source – Herodotus, Histories, Book II, 5th century BC

CASE STUDY

Mesopotamians invented the 12 signs of the zodiac we still use today.

The Zodiac

The Mesopotamians were very keen star-gazers and kept very detailed records, in the form of clay tablets, of the movements of stars and planets across the night sky. When Mesopotamian astronomer-priests divided the night sky into 12 equal parts around 500 BC, and identified each part by a different star constellation, the **ZODIAC** was born. The constellations they recognised are the basis of modern-day star-signs and **HOROSCOPES**. Just as some people today believe horoscopes can predict the future, so did the Mesopotamians:

*'O great ones, gods of the night, ...
O Pleiades, Orion, and the dragon,
O Ursa major, goat (star), and the bison, Stand by, and then, In the divination which I am making,
In the lamb which I am offering,
Put truth for me.'*

Source – Prayer to the gods of the night, Early-2nd millenium BC

Lasting Legacy Glossary

Arabic	Language of the Arabs		a person's future
bracket	Board that runs between and is fixed to two things	**magi**	Three wise men from the east who bought gifts to the infant Jesus
constellation	A group of stars that form a pattern	**tribute**	Payment made by one state or ruler to another
divination	Seeking knowledge from the stars or through magic	**zodiac**	Twelve groups of stars, each of which is linked to a human or animal figure
horoscope	A prediction about		

Index

MESOPOTAMIA TIMELINE

COMMUNITIES 9,000-5,000 BC

9,000 BC
*First animals and plants
are domesticated from the wild.*

8,000 BC
*First known village is established
in Jarmo.*

PRE-SUMERIANS 5,000–3,500 BC

5,000 BC
First labour and first religious shrines.

4,700 BC
Pottery-making is first practised.

3,900 BC
First evidence of temples.

SUMERIANS 3,500–1,900 BC

3,500 BC
*Sumerians settle near the
Euphrates River. The Temple at
Eridu is built.*

3,000 BC
*The pictograph and cuneiform
writing systems are introduced.
Wooden wheels are invented.*

2,334–2,150 BC
Sargon I begins the Akkadian rule.

BABYLONIANS AND ASSYRIANS 1,792–539 BC

1,800–1,170 BC
Old Babylonian period.

1,728–1,685 BC
*Hammurabi gains control of most
of Mesopotamia. He introduces
the Code of Laws.*

1,600–1,100 BC
*Staggered periods of Hittite and Kassite
rule over Mesopotamia.*

1,200-612 BC
Assyrian period.

714–681 BC
Reign of Sennacherib.

668–626 BC
Reign of Ashurbanipal.

612 BC *Fall of Nineveh.*

612–539 BC
Neo-Babylonian Period.

630–562 BC
*Reign of Nebuchadnezzar.
Legend says he built the Hanging
Gardens of Babylon.*

539 BC *Fall of Babylon.*